Anonymus

Souvenir Festival Hymns

Anonymus

Souvenir Festival Hymns

ISBN/EAN: 9783743341098

Manufactured in Europe, USA, Canada, Australia, Japa

Cover: Foto ©Thomas Meinert / pixelio.de

Manufactured and distributed by brebook publishing software
(www.brebook.com)

Anonymus

Souvenir Festival Hymns

Souvenir
Festival Hymns

BOSTON
FREE RELIGIOUS ASSOCIATION
1899

Note.

It has been a common prejudice that the graces of Art, the charms of Song, belong especially to the old mythologic forms of faith. But everything in its time was new, and it is the young, fresh life of freedom and love that sings most rapturously. So Free Religion, while not casting away old songs which still express the universal thought, has felt the need of its own expression.

At the yearly Festival of the Free Religious Association it has been the custom to sing hymns adapted to our broad, liberal views.

Many of these were written especially for these occasions ; some of them have already been published in other collections ; but we feel that those actually written for or sung at our Festivals will form a welcome Souvenir of these occasions devoted to our Third purpose — developing "fellowship in the spirit." Such a collection may also lead in the future to a larger collection of songs which express the freest religion in the sweetest strains.

E. D. C.

Contents.

✿

7

Souvenir Festival Hymns

Festival Hymns

❖

"*The Goodly Fellowship of the Prophets.*"

Tune,—"Hummel."

FROM age to age the prophets rise,
    Still in unbroken line ;
Above the passing centuries
    Like beacon-lights they shine.

Through differing accents of the lip
    One message they proclaim ;
One growing bond of fellowship,
    Above all names, one Name.

They witness to one heritage,
    One Spirit's quickening breath ;
One widening reign, from age to age,
    Of freedom and of faith.

Their kindling power our souls confess ;
    Though dead they speak to-day :
How great the cloud of witnesses
    Encompassing our way !

Through every race, in every clime,
    One song shall yet be heard:
Move onward in thy course sublime,
    O everlasting Word!

— *F. L. Hosmer.*

Written for Festival, F. R. A.,
    June 2, 1899.

" *Oh, How I Love Thy Law.* "

Tune,—"Auld Lang Syne."

❦

FATHER, we come not as of old,
Distrustful of Thy Law,
Hoping to find Thy seamless robe
Marred by some sudden flaw,—
Some rent to let Thy glory through
And make our darkness shine,
If haply thus our souls may know
What power and grace are Thine.

14

Thy seamless robe conceals Thee not
　　From earnest hearts and true ;
The glory of Thy perfectness
　　Shines all its texture through ;
And on its trailing hem we read,
　　As Thou dost linger near,
The message of a love more deep
　　Than any depth of fear.

And so no more our hearts shall plead
　　For miracle and sign,
Thy order and Thy faithfulness
　　Are all in all divine :

These are Thy revelation vast
From earliest days of yore,
These are our confidence and peace,—
We cannot wish for more.

—*John W. Chadwick.*

May 30, 1873.

"*Consider the Lilies, how they Grow !*"

Tune,—"Missionary Hymn."

HE hides within the lily
 A strong and tender care
That wins the earth-born atoms
 To glory of the air ;
He weaves the shining garments
 Unceasingly and still,
Along the quiet waters,
 In niches of the hill.

We linger at the vigil
  With him who bent the knee
To watch the old-time lilies
  In distant Galilee ;
And still the worship deepens
  And quickens into new,
As brightening down the ages
  God's secret thrilleth through.

O Toiler of the lily,
  Thy touch is in the Man !
No leaf that dawns to petal
  But hints the angel-plan.
The flower-horizons open !
  The blossom vaster shows !

18

We hear Thy wide worlds echo,—
  See how the lily grows !

Shy yearnings of the savage,
  Unfolding thought by thought,
To holy lives are lifted,
  To visions fair are wrought ;
The races rise and cluster,
  Transfigurations fall,
Man's chaos blooms to beauty,
  Thy purpose crowning all !

          —William C. Gannett.

May 30, 1873.

"*The Light which Lighteth Every Man.*"

Tune,—"Sweet Hour of Prayer."

O LIFE that maketh all things new,—
  The blooming earth, the thoughts
    of men !
Our pilgrim feet, wet with thy dew,
  In gladness hither turn again.
From hand to hand the greeting flows,
  From eye to eye the signals run,
From heart to heart the bright hope glows ;
  The lovers of the Light are one.

One in the freedom of the Truth,
   One in the joy of paths untrod,
One in the soul's perennial youth,
   One in the larger thought of God ;
The freer step, the fuller breath,
   The wide horizon's grander view,
The sense of life that knows no death,
   The Life that maketh all things new.

              — Samuel Longfellow.

May 29, 1874.

The Glory that Remains.

"If that which is done away was glorious, much more that which remaineth is glorious."

Tune,—"Autumn."

FAIRER grows the earth each morning
  To the eyes that watch aright ;
Every vision is a dawning
  Of some marvel come to light,

Of some unsuspected glory
  Waiting in the old and plain ;
Traveler ne'er told the story ,
  Of such wonders as remain.

As we seek — the quest is duty —
  Inward toward the heart of things,
Everywhere the gate called Beauty
  Fresh across the pathway swings ;
And we enter, foolish mortals,
  Thinking now His throne to find,
Just to gaze on grander portals,—
  Still the Temple lies behind !

23

O my miracles ! you flowers,
  Laughing secrets in my eyes !
Well I know the Heavenly Powers
  Hide from me your best surprise.
O dear brothers 'neath the flowers,
  Glory that was torn away !
Vanished faces light these hours
  More than all the shining May.

Faith I love ! I love you deeper
  That to lose you would be gain ;
Seed may perish, if the reaper
  Comes home singing after pain.

All our creeds are hinting only
  Of a Faith of nobler strain,—
God is living! Who feels lonely
  With the glories that remain?

—William C. Gannett.

Sung at the Social Donation Festival,
May 29, 1874.

25

.

E Pluribus Unum.

Tune,—" Marlow."

M ANY in one, our fathers said,
Many in one, say we ;
Of different creeds, of differing forms,
Love brings us unity.

Let Science scan the open page
Of sky and sea and land,

And tell the secrets written there
By Time's mysterious hand.

Let Art reveal the inner thought
In Nature's forms of grace,
And feel God's presence everywhere,
See everywhere his face.

Let Faith attune the hidden strings
That Science cannot sound,
And Future, Past and Present bind
In one harmonious round.

From each, from all, may life outflow,

To each and all flow in :

It needs us all to swell the chords

Of life's triumphant hymn.

— *Ednah D. Cheney.*

Social Donation Festival, F. R. A.,
June 1, 1877;
and October, 1884.

Light.

Tune,—"Old Hundred."

HAIL to the sun that never sets,
But holds its heavenly place for aye,
And in the soul of man begets,
Age after age, a growing day !

Hail to the light that is the same
For Christian, Paynim, Jew, and Greek,
And, varying not with various names,
Is light for all that truly seek !

Blow, winds of thought ! to clear our skies
That vex the light with darkening change !
No more let clouds the day disguise,
No more man's heart to man be strange.

— D. A. Wasson.

Social Donation Festival, F. R. A.,
June 1, 1877.

In Memoriam.

" Green Pastures and Still Waters."

CLEAR in memory's silent reaches
    Lie the pastures I have seen,
Greener than the sun-lit spaces
    Where the May has flung her green :
Needs no sun and needs no star-light
    To illume these fields of mine,
For the glory of dead faces
    Is the sun, the stars, that shine.

More than one I count my pastures
  As my life-path groweth long ;
By their quiet waters straying
  Oft I lay me, and am strong.
And I call each by its giver ;
  And the dear names bring to them
Glory as from shining faces
  In some new Jerusalem.

Yet, O well I can remember,
  Once I called my pastures, Pain ;
And the waters were a torrent
  Sweeping through my life amain !
Now I call them Peace and Stillness,
  Brightness of all Happy Thought,

Where I linger for a blessing
   From my faces that are naught.

Naught ? I know not. If the Power
   Maketh thus his pastures green,
Maketh thus his quiet waters,
   Out of waste, his heavens serene,
I can trust the mighty Chemist
   Of the May-lands and the soul,
And the faces of my dead ones
   Pledge no waste within the Whole !

                —*William C. Gannett.*

Festival, F. R. A.,
at Parker Memorial Meeting-House,
May 27, 1881,
and June 1, 1877.

Apple - Blossoms.

AS the apple-tree to-day
Blossoms in the sun of May,
Yet long months must work and wait
Till it bear its precious freight,
Till the golden fruit appear,
Noblest harvest of the year,—

So to-day we sing our song,
Speak our word ; but, waiting long,
Rain and sunshine meet our need,
Thought shall ripen into deed,
Love, with faith and beauty rife,
Slowly bring the fruits of life.

— *Ednah D. Cheney.*

May 27, 1881,
and May 28, 1885.

Our October Supper.

CREEDS and ceremonies perish,
     Fallen leaves that must decay :
Ours the living Truth to cherish ;
     She can never pass away.

Freedom holds her firm dominion
     In this land of equal rights :
Science spreads her mighty pinion
     Every day for higher flights.

Faith in Man grows stronger, clearer,
    As we see our neighbors' worth :
Duty's ancient laws are dearer ;
    New ones have their holy birth.

Ours to keep this sacred treasure
    Open for the use of all ;
In the hour of social pleasure
    Hear the Future's bugle-call !

— F. M. Holland.

October, 1884.

" *Watchman, what of the Night ?* "

Tune,—"Hamburg."

❦

OUT of the dark, the circling sphere
　　Is rounding onward to the light :
We see not yet the full day here,
　　But we do see the paling night.

And Hope, that lights her fadeless fires ;
　　And Faith, that shines, a heavenly will ;
And Love, that courage reinspires,—
　　These stars have been above us still.

O sentinels ! whose tread we heard
　Through long hours when we could not
　　　see,
Pause now ; exchange with cheer the word,
　The unchanging watchword, Liberty !

Look backward, how much has been won !
　Look round, how much is yet to win !
The watches of the night are done :
　The watches of the day begin.

— Samuel Longfellow.

December Supper, F. R. A.,
　December 10, 1884.

Past, Present, Future.

Tune,—"Russian Hymn."

O EARTH, thy past is crowned and
consecrated
With its reformers, speaking yet, though
dead ;
Who unto strife and toil and tears were
fated,
Who unto fiery martyrdoms were led.

O Earth, thy present, too, is crowned with
splendor
By its Reformers battling in the strife ;

Friends of humanity, stern, strong, and
    tender,
  Making the world more hopeful with
    their life.

O Earth, thy future shall be great and
    glorious,
  With its Reformers toiling in the van,
Till Truth and Love shall reign o'er all
    victorious,
  And earth be given to freedom and to
    man.

                —T. L. Harris.

December Supper, F. R. A.,
  December 10, 1884.

A Hymn.

Tune,—"Antioch."

OUR life is full of love and light
　　Because our aims are high.
In Freedom's service we unite :
　　Her reign supreme is high.

Thy growth, O Science, gives us joy !
　　Thy victory is ours !
March on, and all thy foes destroy !
　　We bless thy mighty powers.

No holy sacrament we ken
   Save that of doing good :
Our faith is in our fellow-men,
   Our creed is brotherhood.

We love this world of life and light ;
   We drink its gladness in :
The morning drives away the night,
   And golden days begin !

— *F. M. Holland.*

May 28, 1885.

Free Religious Welcome.

Tune,—" Coronation."

TO-NIGHT in full accord we meet,
 With loving hearts and free :
In equal fellowship we greet,
 In loving charity.

Bring with you every sacred book,
 The Gods you love and trust,
The kindling hopes that heavenward look,
 The memories of the just ;

The sacred reverence for law,
   The earnest search for truth,
The lessons that from age we draw,
   The prophecies of youth.

Come one, come all, who come in love !
   Our church is wide and free,
Free as God's glorious heaven above,
   Wide as Humanity !

                —Ednah D. Cheney.

May 29, 1896.

45

The Law of Liberty.

Tune,—"Rock of Ages."

THOU, whose name is blazoned forth
　　On our banner's gleaming fold,
Freedom ! thou whose sacred worth
　　Never yet has half been told,
Often have we sung of thee,
Dear to us as dear can be.

But to-night we sing of one
   Older, graver far than thou,
With the seal of time begun
   Stamped upon her awful brow :
Freedom, latest born of time,
Knowest thou her form sublime ?

She is Duty : in her hand
   Is a sceptre heaven-brought ;
Hers the accent of command,
   Hers the dreadful, mystic Ought :
Hers upon us all to lay
Heavier burdens every day.

But her bondage is so sweet !

And her burdens make us strong ;
Wings they seem to weary feet,

Laughter to our lips and song :
Freedom, make us free to speed
Wheresoever she may lead.

—John W. Chadwick.

May 29, 1896.

Life of Ages.

Telemann's Chant.

❦

LIFE of Ages, richly poured,
  Love of God, unspent and free,
Flowing in the prophet's word
And the people's liberty !

Never was to chosen race
  That unstinted tide confined ;

Thine is every time and place,
  Fountain sweet of heart and mind.

Breathing in the thinker's creed,
  Pulsing in the hero's blood,
Nerving simplest thought and deed,
  Freshening time with truth and good,—

Consecrating art and song,
  Holy book and pilgrim track;
Hurling floods of tyrant wrong
  From the sacred limits back,—

Life of Ages, richly poured,
  Love of God, unspent and free,
Flow still in the prophet's word
  And the people's liberty !

— Samuel Johnson.

Festival, F. R. A.,
  May 28, 1898.

Raphael's Saint Cecilia at Bologna.

❦

A CHALLENGE of celestial art
    Doth through the æther fall,
And, like a well-tuned harp, my heart
    Makes answer to its call.

The breath of God is in this sky,
    So limpid and so blue;
His radiance, streaming from on high,
    Lights up the world anew.

The music of the circling spheres
   That hasten not, nor rest,
Insensible to mortal ears,
   Wakes echoes in my breast.

And thus it whispers, low and sweet :
   " The Highest draweth nigh ;
Sing, brothers, sing ! with measure meet
   Salute Heaven's majesty."

           —Julia Ward Howe.

Written for Festival, F. R. A.,
   June 2, 1899.

Festival Mottoes

❦

LET knowledge grow from more to more,
   But more of reverence in us dwell,
   That mind and soul, according well,
May make one music as before,
But vaster.   — *Tennyson.*

   May 30, 1873.

✿

To see a World in a grain of sand,
   And a Heaven in a wild flower,
Hold Infinity in the palm of your hand,
   And Eternity in an hour.
            —*William Blake.*
May 29, 1874.

Devoutly look, and naught
But wonders shall pass by thee ;
Devoutly read, and then
All books shall edify thee ;
Devoutly speak, and men
Devoutly listen to thee ;
Devoutly act, and then
The strength of God acts through thee.

— Rueckert's "Wisdom of the Brahmins."

May 29, 1874.

With wider view come loftier goal !
With broader light, more good to see !
With freedom, more of self-control,
With knowledge, deeper reverence be !

Anew we pledge ourselves to Thee,
  To follow where thy Truth shall lead :
Afloat upon its boundless sea,
  Who sails with God is safe indeed.
                    — *Samuel Longfellow.*
June 2, 1876.

Our God ! our God ! Thou shinest here,
  Thine own this latter day ;
To us Thy radiant steps appear,
  Here leads thy glorious way !

Thou comest near ; Thou standest by ;
  Our work begins to shine ;
Thou dwellest with us mightily,—
  On come the years divine !
                    — *T. H. Gill.*
June 2, 1876.

Deep is the wild sea's bottom sweep,
But hundred thousand times more deep
    Is the vast sweep
Of thy great pity growing ;
It reaches from the stars' high throne
Unto the bottomless ocean's moan ;
    A comb o'erflown
With the sweetest honey flowing.

June 1, 1877.

Our little systems have their day,
    They have their day, and cease to be ;
    They are but broken lights of Thee,
And Thou, O Lord, art more than they.
                      — Tennyson.

Unless you understand an author's ignorance, conclude yourself ignorant of his understanding. — *Coleridge.*

❦

A leaf may hide the largest star
   From Love's uplifted eye ;
A mote of prejudice out-bar
   A world of Charity.
           —John B. Tabb.

❦

Thus Faith, cast out of barren creeds,
   Shall rest in emblems of her own ;
Beauty, still springing from Decay,
   The cross-wood budding to the crown.
           —Julia Ward Howe.

He who feels contempt for any living thing
Hath faculties within his soul which he hath
never used,
And thought with him is in its infancy.

—*Wordsworth.*

He who begins by loving Christianity better than Truth will continue by loving his own sect or party better than Christianity, and end by loving himself best of all.

— *Coleridge.*

*9 7 8 3 7 4 3 3 4 1 0 9 8 *